CW00765494

SOUTH OF FRANCE

A BOOK OF DAYS
SARA MIDDA

WORKMAN PUBLISHING
NEW YORK

Copyright© 1993, 1990, by Sara Midda
All rights reserved.

No portion of this diary may be reproduced
mechanically, electronically, or by any other means including
photocopying without written permission from the publisher.

Published simultaneously in Canada
by Thomas Allen & Son Ltd.

Workman Publishing
708 Broadway
New York, NY 10003

Printed in Japan

9 8 7 6 5 4 3

This Diary Belongs To...

Alice Malone

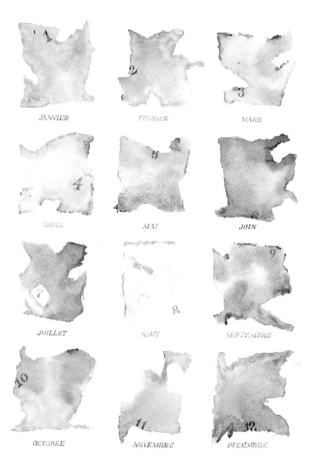

JANVIER

FEVRIER

MARS

AVRIL

MAI

JUIN

JUILLET

AOUT

SEPTEMBRE

OCTOBRE

NOVEMBRE

DECEMBRE

oing out with sean Hancher
Lay really like it nice guys

1

New Year's Day

2

3

4

5

GozzoS . Got I.D'd

6

7

8

9

10

11 chatted to the Vision from Warner
Tom ~~Booth~~ Moore. He borght me a drin
Torch
worked

12

13

14

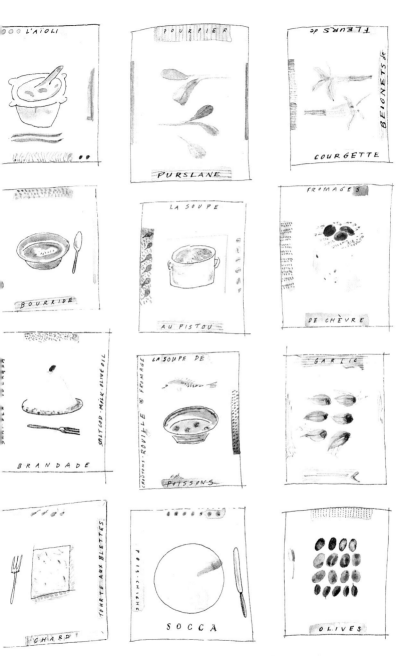

15

Martin Luther King Jr.'s Birthday

16

17 V. Goodlooking

18 Met Tom at torch again he really likes me but has G. friend gave me his E.Mail Adr? dead end really innit!

19 worked got sent hone because was too ill. Truth is, I was just gutted that Tom has girlfriend, cause I like him.

20 Templation island. worked.

21 worked

worked 6-10.

22

Sent tom an email on sofs computer, I really fancy him and can't stop thinking about him, feel guilty cause I am going out with sean.

23

went to whatch unbreakable at warners, No my life dosn't just evolve around boys. but was hoping tom would b there.

24

Torch - Tom was there, he loved the email, I pulled him and he walked me home and left my house at 6:00 AM was lovely.

25

work 6-10 boring because no friends there.

26

Birmingham shopping with lizzie + mum, buying curling tongs + cloths.

27

must Dump sean. can't stand cheating.
Tom met me after work came to mine left at 1 mmm said hed call

28

le PAIN

bread la tête d'Aix

sablé

au chocolat

La charleston niçois

La couronne

Pain aux olives. Son La Fougasse

la baguette

BOULANGERIE

la main de Nice. la lune

Fougassettes - Anchois Michettes à la tomate

le restaurant

l'épis.

Grissini

les rioutes

le pain d'Aix.

finished with sean, wasn't
good, he was very tramatic 30
going to Lough on Thurs
nite, withbed I like torch,
t always makes me feel 31
better Tom might be there

↗

le phoned and came
round, we went
fer a walke and a
drive. MMM I like
we are real silly
togcther.

Th
1

Fr
2

S
3

Su
4

M
5

Tu
6

W
7

Thu

8

9

10

11

12

Lincoln's Birthday

13

14

Valentine's Day

Thu
15

Fr
16

S
17

Su
18

19

20

21

7:00 am

11:00 am

1:30 pm

4:00 pm

10:30 pm

22

Washington's Birthday

23

24

25

26

27

28/29

1

2

3

4

5

6

7

8

9

10

11

12

13

14

15

___

16

___

17

St. Patrick's Day

___

18

___

19

___

20

___

21

UPINETTI

22

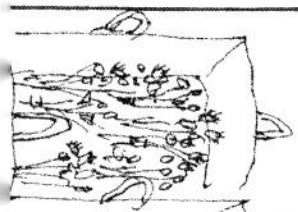

RNATIONS-
, white, magenta,
v. Mottled, striped

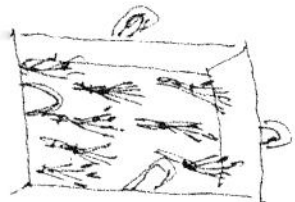

23

REESIA

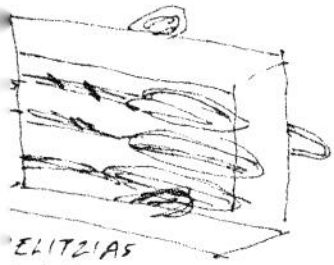

24

ELITZIAS
ed like ears

25

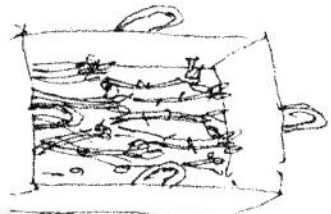

MARYLLIS BUDS

26

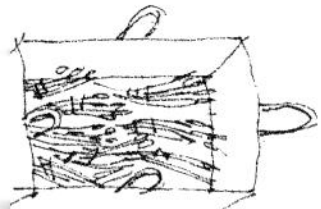

HIN IRISES

27

NCHES OF
AFFODILS

28

29

_____

30

_____

31

_____

fresh herbs

MESCLUN/MESCLUM – from latin miscellanea
Typically Niçois mix of young salad plants.

MESCLUM de PROVENCE

MODE DE CULTURE

Ce mélange est à semer de février
à septembre. Les jeunes plantes
d'un mois et demi à deux mois,
coupés et assaisonnés ensemble
vous donneront le délicieux MESCLUM.

Cette pochette contient :
ROQUETTE CULTIVÉE . LAITUE A
COUPER FEUILLE DE CHÊNE . CHICORÉE
FRISÉE . CHICORÉE SAUVAGE. LAITUE
À ROMAINE BLONDE MARAÎCHÈRE.
CHICOREE DE TREVISE .

courgettes long

courgettes round

1

2

3

4

5

6

7

8

9

10

11

12

13

14

twelve fresh eggs, and one for 'la chance'.

4 minute hard boiled Eggs for picnic.

Paint eggs for Easter-egg hunt ?

Menu of an Artesia Mac . 1806

7 am: Anchovies, turnips, onions & quality wine
9.3am: Cheese, watered wine,
Midday: Thick vegetable soup & an ;
2pm: Salad with olive oil & garlic, cheese :
4pm: Piece of bread + a glass of wine
7pm , Soup, meat or vegetable, and a glass
            of wine.

Fresh Eggs

15

16

17

18

19

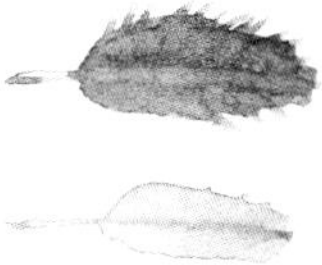

20

21

22

23

24

25

26

27

28

29

30

1

2

3

4

5

6

7

Bank of marjoram - in flower.
Dandelions ?
Salad burnet
Alium (flower)
Wonderful scented Broom
Fennel - young shoots.
Scabious
Drifts of poppies that bleed into the vineyard
Piercing blue flax /linum.
Lathyrus
Spurge
Tiny snails clinging to grass
Convolvulus - thinly striped petals
Small wild gladiolii
Santolina - grey/green stems. Faded yellow flowers.
Cistus (pungent scent always reminds me of here)
White Roses
Fig trees - small ones.

8

9

10

11

12

13

14

15

16

17

18

19

20

21

22

23

24

25

26

27

28

29

30

Traditional Memorial Day

31

1

sardines salées

2

3

4

5

6

7

8

_____

9

_____

10

_____

11

_____

12

_____

13

_____

14

JUNE

15

16

17

18

19

20

21

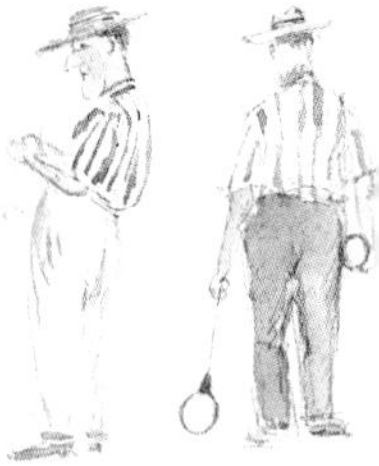

Early evening. Playing BOULES (Pétanque)

22

23

24

25

26

27

28

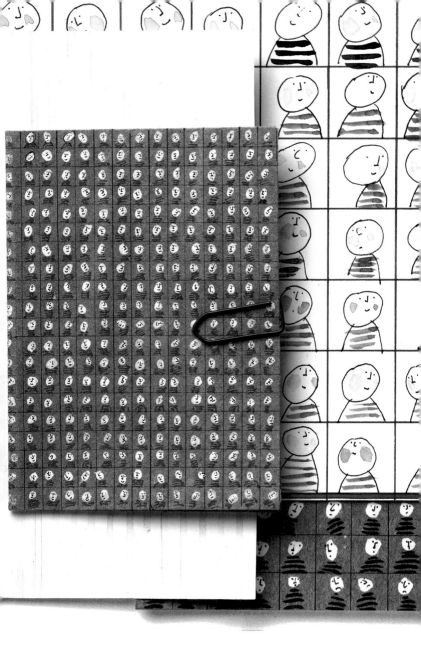

29

30

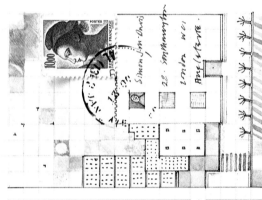

FOR YOUR / + 2 + 3 + 4 + 5 + 6 + 7 + 8 = 36 th birthday

LURE OF STATIONERY SHOP. NOTEBOOKS, REPERTOIRES, FOLDERS,
ALMOND SCENTED GLUE, PAPER- CHECKED, LINED, SQUARED. SOFT COLOURS,
ABOUT TO SEARCH FOR YOUR PRESENT. GLUE ↓

JULY

1

Canada Day (Canada)

2

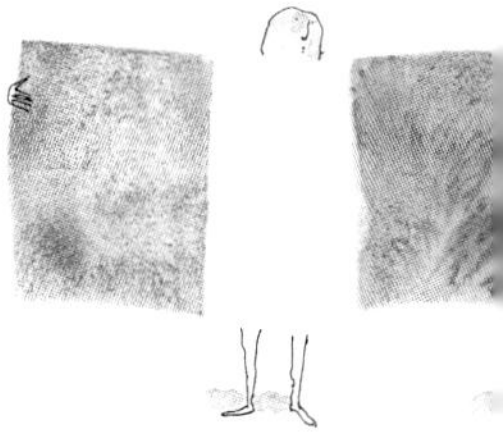

3

4

Independence Day

5

6

7

8

9

10

11

12

Blue SKY

13

14

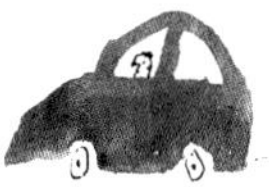

Favorite French Car.

15

16

17

18

19

20

21

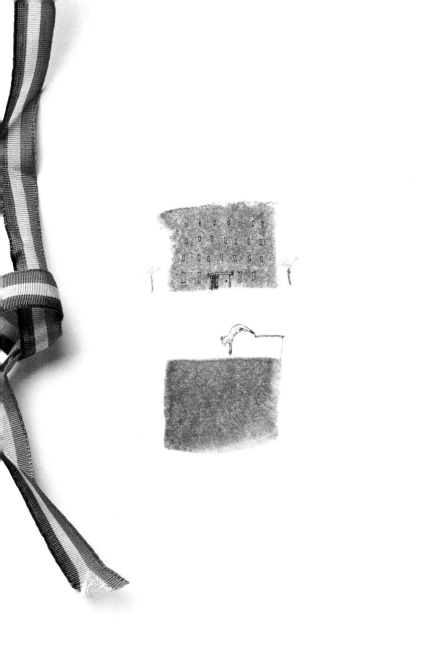

22

___

23

___

24

___

25

___

26

___

27

___

28

29

30

31

citrons

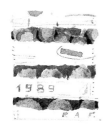

1989

R.A.F.

Ail. Eschalottes

NAVET   ESCAROLE
                B'HIVE

        LAROTTE
        LES 100 g . . .   CHICON
                                BLANC
                                B'HIVER
                                Ja Kg

KADIS LONG   BATAVIA
FLAMBOYANT   ROUGE
                    LES 100 gms

COURGE

Poulet
25 f PIECE

AU NECESSAIRE

Assortiment
d'Articles
de menage

BOXES OF CORNICHONS.
FIGS WRAPPED IN THEIR LEAF.

EXHAUSTION

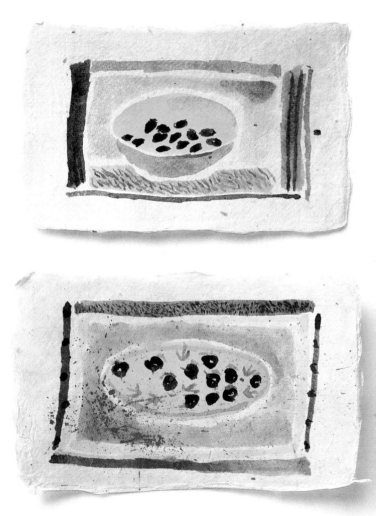

1

2

3

4

5

6

7

8

9

10

11

12

13

14

15

16

17

18

19

20

21

22

_____

23

_____

24

_____

25

_____

26

_____

27

_____

28

29

30

31

1

2

3

4

5

6

7

8

9

10

11

12

13

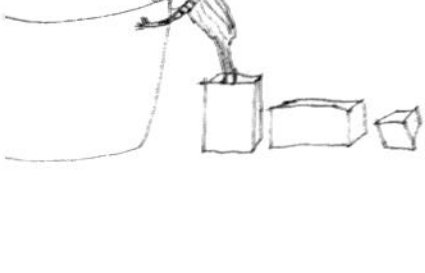

14

15

16

17

18

19

20

21

22

23

bago flower

24

25

26

ning fishy

27

s ripe peach —

28

29

30

Olives Niçoises

Olives au Citron
Fenouil

Noires
Façon Grèce

Vertes
Picholines de
Provence

Noires de Nyons

Vertes cassées
des Baux

Sauce Escabèche

Olives cassées
aux herbes

Olives aux
Herbes de Provence

Farcies Poivrons

Noires à l'ail
et basilic.

1

2

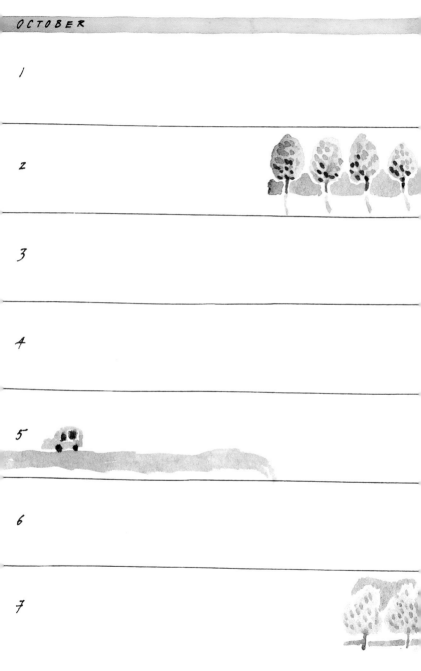

3

4

5

6

7

8

9

10

11

12

Traditional Columbus Day

13

14

GRAND CAFE · DE SID

DEGUSTATION de COQUILLAGES

Cuisss Grenouilles
Escargots
Bouquet
            Cosvsttss
Pain de SEIGLE
Crevettss Grisss
Scampi

des Huitres
Specialts
Vertes de Claires
Fines de Claires
Citrons
Amandes de Mer
Oursins
Biqormeaux
Palourdes
Tovteaux
Crevsttss
Langoustss

squ à 21h30   Maison de...

POUR TOUTES OUVERTURES de COQU

Moulrs - Bouziques
        Espagne
    Bouchot
    Supsr Bouchots

15

16

17

Panaché
maison

60.10

18

0.50

19

VIVE LA VIE!
Assiette de
MOULES

NET
11

20

21

22

23

24

25

26

27

28

29

30

31

Halloween

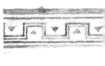

1

2

3

4

5

6   *Cafe de L'Unive*

7

BAR des AMIS

Expresso

hard-boiled eggs

m A N
IN
a beret

Paper table cloths →

8

9

10

11
Veterans Day
Remembrance Day (Canada)

12

13

14

BAR

AFE

AFE COU

Brasserie

ou Souleù

la PAIX

CAFÉ

22

23

24

25

26

27

28

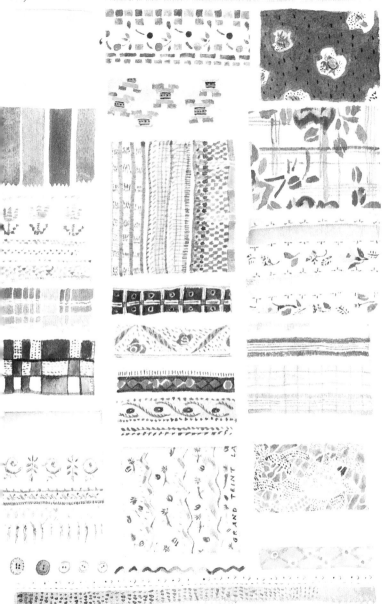

GRAND TEINT LA

29

30

Figs

1

2

3

4

5

6

7

8

9

10

11

12

13

14

15

16

17

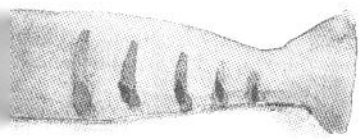

18

19

20

21

tartes aux Fruits

tarte aux fraises

Dôme chocolat

Citron

Baba au Rhum

Palmier

Panier

Citron

Al pezzo

surprise au chocolat

22

23

24

25

Christmas

26

Boxing Day (Canada)

27

28

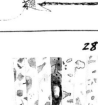

29

30

31

Names and Addresses

A

B

C

D

E

F

G

H—1

J

K

M

N

Q-R

5

$\mathcal{T}$

$u-v$

WXYZ